*For Lauren, who has grown into
an exceptional young woman.*

Chapter One

It started out like any other day. Nobody wants to believe that. People say, "Well, you must have missed something," or "How could you not know?" I think it makes them feel better. I think it makes them feel that if they had been me, if they'd been in the same place at the same time, they would have somehow done it better than I did.

I know I didn't do it perfectly, but I did the best that I could—at least I did something—and I hope that was enough.

That day, Mac was already at the old lodge in the park when I came up the hill. I could see her up on the balcony off the main level. On the front of the old building, the door is at ground level and you can walk right inside. On the back, because the lodge is built into the hill, the main part is two stories in the air, so the balcony is maybe fifteen or sixteen feet off the ground.

We weren't even supposed to be on the balcony—nobody was—because there were "issues" with some of the decking boards. That's city-government-speak meaning some of the wood was rotting. There was a chain blocking the bottom of the outside stairs. A yellow

Keep Out, Danger sign hung from the heavy metal links.

An old lady with a walker could have stepped over that chain. To keep kids out of somewhere, you have to do better than just a droopy chain. And those *Keep Out, Danger* signs? They just make some people more determined to get in. People like Mac, for example. Okay, and me. Call it teenage rebellion. That's what my mother calls it.

So, anyway, Mac was there first, up on the rotten wood balcony, on top of the railing. Yeah, I mean on the railing, as in walking across it like she was that guy who wanted to walk over the Grand Canyon on a tightrope, although Mac was on a six-inch-wide piece of wood instead. Now, see, some people would say *that* was a sign, but I don't think it was. Mac was always getting up on that railing, holding out her arms and walking from one end of the balcony all the way to the other end.

Sometimes she'd close her eyes. Once she stopped in the middle and pretended she was jumping rope. She scared the piss out of me every time she got up there, but I knew not to let on that it bothered me, because if I did, then Mac would do something more over the top and maybe she *would* fall.

I stepped over the chain and went up the stairs, getting to the top just as Mac got to the end of the railing. My heart was pounding in my chest, the way it always did when she got up there, but I just looked at her with a half smile and said, "Hey, Mac."

"Hey, Daniel," she said. She jumped down and pointed at the Tim's bag I was holding. "What've you got?"

I opened the top, and she looked inside. Then she looked at me. "Okay, so what do you want?" she said, glaring at me through her bangs.

I pulled the bag away and went over to sit against the wall of the building. "I don't want anything," I said. "Jeez, Mac, it's just a freakin' donut."

"Yeah, well, since when do you buy me donuts?"

"I don't," I said. "But they've got this contest thing they're doing and I won a chocolate glazed donut, which I don't like but you do, and so I figured I'd give it to you. But if you don't want it, I can just find a squirrel or something to eat it instead."

Mac came over and sat down beside me, bumping me with her shoulder. "You are such a girl sometimes, Danny Boy," she said with a grin. She took the chocolate glazed donut out of the bag and I pulled out the dutchie I'd bought for myself, and we sat there taking turns drinking the coffee I'd gotten too.

So maybe there was a sign after all. Maybe the fact that I'd won a stupid donut at Tim's—and believe me, I never win anything—and of all the donuts they sell, it was Mac's all-time favorite. Maybe that did mean something. At the time, I thought it was just a donut. Maybe I was wrong.

"So where were you all day?" she asked after the coffee and both donuts were gone.

I leaned my head back against the rough shingles and closed my eyes. "Helping my mother clean out the basement," I said. I wouldn't have said that to anyone else, but I knew Mac wouldn't make fun of me.

"That's nice," she said. I felt her lean back against the wall too.

"You going over to the school later to work on your composition?" I asked after a moment. "Hanson said he'd be there so we can get into the music room."

"Nope. I'm done."

I opened my eyes wide and turned to look at her. "What do you mean you're done? How the hell can you be done?"

Mac's face was tipped up to the sky like she was soaking up the sun, except there really wasn't any. About two weeks ago she'd suddenly cut off all her long red hair for a short, chopped cut with messy bangs. I was still getting used to it.

"I mean I'm done. *Fini. Completo.* I wrote out the rest of the music. I recorded it. I burned the CD. I'm done."

The composition project was half of our term music mark. I couldn't believe Mac was finished while I was still struggling to get the notes on paper— that is, if I'd actually had any music in my head to write down.

I let my head fall back against the wall again and stared up into the gray April sky. "Friday, you weren't any further ahead than I am. What did you do? Spend the whole day in the music room?"

I felt her shrug beside me. "Last night, mostly," she said.

"You lie," I said, letting my eyes slide sideways so I could see her without moving my head. "There was a dance last night, so Hanson would have been in the gym making sure none of the guys on the hockey team were drinking or putting their hands down some girl's thong."

Her lips twitched with a hint of a smile. "Great visual, Danny Boy. But just so you know, some of us don't go for the butt-floss look."

I reached over and gave her shoulder a shove. "Yeah, well, thanks for *that* visual, Mac."

She grinned, but she kept her head against the brown shingles, and her eyes stayed closed.

I stretched my legs across the wooden deck and slid down until the back of my head was the only thing still against the building. "Seriously, how'd you get into the music room?"

"Maybe I broke in. Maybe I picked the lock with a paperclip and a toothpick. Maybe I swiped pointy-faced Mrs. Robinson's keys. Or maybe…"

She let the word hang in the air for a long moment. "Maybe Mr. Hanson went in to get a guitar, because some suck-up suggested he sit in with the band for a song. And maybe he didn't lock up behind himself the way he should have."

She opened her eyes then and jumped to her feet. "C'mon, Danny Boy," she said, jerking her head toward the steps. "Let's go."

"What are you on?" I said, squinting up at her. "I spent all day hauling boxes of crap that came from my grand-parents' house out of the basement of my parents' house. Leave me alone. Let me sleep."

I closed my eyes, but she bent down, grabbed my arm and hauled me to my feet. Mac was kinda short—she only came up to my shoulder—but she was strong. I could feel her fingers digging into my wrist through my sweatshirt, and I pretty much had to go with her, because she wasn't letting go and I was going to fall on my ass going down those stairs if I didn't keep up.

Chapter Two

"Where are we going?" I said as Mac cut across the grass, headed for the hill that led down to the street.

She'd let go of my arm, and I was following her, mostly because what the hell else did I have to do on an almost Saturday night?

"I wanna show you something," she said.

"Show me what?"

She turned around and started walking backward. "See, the thing is, Danny Boy," she said, making a big sweeping movement with one hand, "when someone wants to show you something, you have to actually see it."

"So where's everyone else tonight?" I asked, partly because I really did want to know, and partly because I knew she wasn't going to tell me where we were going and I didn't want her to think I cared about knowing that much. Yeah, I know that's warped.

She pressed her fingers to both sides of her head and squeezed her eyes shut. She was still walking backward, and I don't know why she didn't fall, but she didn't. It was just like being up on the railing. "I'm trying, I'm trying," she said, and then she opened her eyes and gave me a big fake shrug. "Sorry, my psychic abilities aren't working at the moment." She looked around. "I think all the trees are screwing with the reception."

"Yeah, ha, ha, ha," I said. She was in a weird mood. Not weird in the way that I should have been worried. I've thought about that a lot too. She was just crazier than she usually was. And no, it wasn't like she'd taken something. That wasn't Mac's thing.

She waited for a red SUV to go by, then shot across the street. I stopped at the curb, looked both ways, and when there were no cars coming, I walked over to her. She stood on the sidewalk shaking her head, but she didn't say anything for once. A lot of the time she called me Gramps because I always waited for the light, or if there were no walk lights, I waited until there weren't any cars coming, unlike Mac, who thought crossing the street was like running some kind of obstacle course.

Me, I still remembered, back in grade six, seeing Kevin Kessler get hit by a car that ignored the red lights and passed the school bus that we'd just gotten off. I was already on the other side of the street, and as I turned to say something to Kevin, the car hit him. He flew through the air, arms reaching like he was trying to grab on to something, his mouth open for a scream that never came out, and landed in the ditch to the left of me. I remember scrambling down the bank through the gravel and the weeds, screaming for someone to come help and trying not to puke, swiping at my face because I didn't want anyone to see me crying.

"Are you going to tell me where you're taking me?" I said as we headed along the sidewalk. I knew it wouldn't do any good to bug her. But I couldn't seem to help doing it anyway. We were going in the general direction of the university.

Was that where we were headed? Mac? Not likely.

Mac acted like I hadn't said anything, which is what she always did when she didn't want to talk about stuff. Since she wasn't going to answer my questions, I just walked along beside her, sneaking little looks at her when I figured she wasn't paying any attention to me.

I liked looking at Mac. She didn't smile that often, but it made her look like some kind of hot supermodel when she did. And she had a great laugh. It made you want to know what was so damn funny when you heard it. Sometimes I tried to make her laugh just because the sound was so freakin' good.

"Why are you looking at me, Danny Boy?" she said all of a sudden.

Busted.

"What makes you think I want to look at your ugly self?" I said, bumping her hip with my own.

She just rolled her eyes and didn't say anything else.

At the corner we crossed over—there weren't any cars coming in either direction—and Mac headed up the hill. I'd pretty much given up on getting her to say anything about where we were headed or why, so I didn't ask again. I just walked beside her and made sure she didn't catch me checking her out again.

We ended up on a little side street about halfway up the hill, in front of a small green house. The yard was partly dug up, and the whole house was surrounded by portable chain-link fence, maybe six feet high.

Mac led me around to the backyard. "Where are you going?" I hissed as I scrambled over the rutted dirt and chewed-up grass that looked like it used to be a driveway. She dragged her fingers along the fence and then stopped so quickly I almost bumped into her. My foot slipped on the muddy ground, and I grabbed a skinny maple tree to keep from ending up on my ass in the dirt.

Mac pulled back a section of the fence like she was pulling back a pop-top and squeezed through the opening she'd made. She kept one hand on the wire, pushing it out so the opening was still there for me. "C'mon, Danny Boy," she said impatiently.

"What are you doing? This is trespassing," I said.

"No, it isn't," she said. "Are you coming or not?" I could see the challenge in her dark eyes, and I knew if I didn't go, then she'd just take off for the house and leave me standing there like some kind of dork.

So what if I got arrested for trespassing? So what if I got a criminal record and didn't get a music scholarship to university and ended up having to wear a baby-blue tuxedo and play the piano at the Starbright Lounge in the Wayfarer Inn six nights a week for all the old ladies who smell like cough drops and the occasional little old man with his pants up under his armpits? It was better than having Mac think I was a wuss.

Chapter Three

I squeezed through the hole in the fence. The back of my sweatshirt got caught for a moment, but I twisted loose and stood up, bending the wire back in place so anyone walking by probably wouldn't notice the gap.

Mac had already picked her way across what was left of the lawn to the rear of the little house. She was doing something at the back door. Oh sure, why not add breaking and entering to trespassing while we were at it? If I was going to have a criminal record, it might as well be a long one.

She got the door open and jammed something into her pocket just as I got to her. "Wait a minute," I said. "You have a key to that door?"

She looked back over her shoulder at me. "Standardized testing was wrong," she said. "The boy does have a few brain cells left." Then she went in, and I followed her.

We were standing in a small hallway at the back of the house. To my right there was a bathroom. I could see a tub, a toilet, a sink in a white cabinet, and some kind of blue tile with flowers on the wall. On the other side, a narrow set of steps led upstairs.

I glared at Mac. "Stop screwing with me," I said. "Whose house is this?"

She was already on her way up the stairs. They were covered in faded gold-colored carpet. "It's mine," she said over her shoulder.

I scrambled up after her. "What do you mean it's yours? How can you have a house?"

She stopped, turned around and leaned forward just a little, so her face was pretty close to mine. "It's mine," she repeated. Then she went the rest of the way up, two steps at a time.

When I got to the top, Mac was in the room to the left. There were only two rooms up there. One took up the left side of the space, and one took up the other side. There wasn't really as much room as you'd think on that floor, because the roof was slanted and it was like standing in a big triangle in a way.

I stopped in the doorway. Mac was in the center of the room, which had been painted pale purple. "So you dragged me over here just so I could see this old house that you'd like to have?"

She shook her head. "I take it back," she said. "There are no functioning brain cells left after all." Then she walked over to me and smacked the top of my head with her hand. "Hello! Is anything working in there?"

I twisted away from her. "Oh yeah, you're really funny, Mac," I said.

She dropped her hand to my shoulder and gave me a small smile. "I brought you here to see this." She gestured to the room. "This is my room."

And then I got it. I don't know why I'd been so slow before. Mac used to live with her grandmother. I didn't know what had happened to her mother or her father, because she wouldn't talk about them ever. I figured they were probably dead.

About six months ago, her grand-mother had a stroke and died in the hospital. Mac had had to go live with her uncle, and because of the spazoid way they work out who goes to what school, she ended up having to switch over to Riverview. I didn't even know what her uncle's real name was, because all she ever called him was The Asshole.

I can remember her walking into homeroom that first morning with Mrs. Robinson, the guidance counselor, and there was just something about the way she stood there, like she didn't care that we were all sneaking looks at her, that made me know I was going to be her friend if she'd let me.

I followed Mac into the bedroom. It was empty except for an air mattress against the end wall with a pillow and a couple of blankets folded all neatly on top. Pretty clear that Mac had been sleeping here some of the time. Or maybe more like a lot of the time.

But the one thing that I saw right away—that I couldn't stop looking at— was the slanted ceiling. It was painted the same pale purple color as the walls, but it was covered with writing, covered, side to side, top to bottom. The whole thing was Mac's small, cramped lettering. I moved closer and started reading bits and pieces. It was all poems and song lyrics, a bunch of stuff I'd never seen before. I was pretty damn sure that Mac had written all of it herself, not copied someone else's stuff.

And it was good. I'm pretty fair at writing music, if you don't count this stupid comp project. But I suck at writing the words. All I can ever come up with is dumb rhymes like "moon" and "June" or "same" and "lame." But Mac was good. No, Mac was great. My fingers were actually itching because I wanted my guitar or a piano so I could start figuring out the notes to go behind the words.

"Jesus, Mac," I whispered. "These are good."

She didn't say anything, and I walked back and forth for at least ten minutes reading what was written up there on the ceiling. Some of it was above my head, and it was getting dark, so I couldn't see it very well. Finally I looked at her. She was sitting on the air mattress, her back against the wall. "You've got all this stuff written down, right?" I said.

She pointed at the slanted ceiling above my head. "Yeah, there," she said.

"No, I mean on paper or on a memory stick or something."

She shook her head.

I pulled a hand back through my hair. "Okay, so first what we have to do is go get a couple of notebooks and some pens. I can start at one end, and you can start at the other. We could do it in two or three days."

"They're tearing this place down tomorrow morning," Mac said softly.

"Shit," I muttered. "Okay. So we'll go get Alex and Ren, and we'll just stay here all night if we have to." I looked around, and it hit me that there was probably no electricity connected anymore if the house was going to be torn down in the morning. I reached over and flipped the light switch.

Nothing.

"All right, copying it all down's not going to work because we can't see to do it." I held out my hands and shook my fingers. They still had that itchy, tingling feeling. Then I remembered that I had my phone in my pocket. "Jesus, I'm so stupid," I said. I pulled out the phone. "I think there's enough light that I can just take pictures of everything." I stepped back and snapped a shot of one small square of the ceiling. I looked at the picture.

No. I was too far away to make out the writing in the image.

"I'm going to have to get closer," I said. I held the phone just a few inches away from the purple paint.

Mac grabbed my arm. "No," she said.

"Are you crazy?" I asked, shaking off her hand. "You can't let this get destroyed. It's good! I mean it."

"Tomorrow it'll be gone, Daniel," she said with a small smile. "There's nothing anybody can do. Let it go. I have."

I looked around. "I don't get it, Mac. Whose house is this now? I mean I know it used to be your grandmother's, right?"

"Mine," she said, letting go of me. "At least it was."

I held out both hands. "I don't understand."

She looked up at all the words scrawled on the ceiling. "Gram left the house to me. She left everything she had to me—not that there was very much.

The thing is, The Asshole is in charge of it all." She shrugged. "He decided it would be better to sell the house and save the money for my education. There wasn't anything I could do— can do. My grandmother's gone. By tomorrow this house will be gone. Everything will be gone. It's too late."

"Too late?" I said. "That's just—"

I didn't get to finish the sentence, because she put one hand on each side of my face and kissed me full on the lips.

Chapter Four

"Jesus, Mac," I managed to mumble before her warm tongue was in my mouth and I pretty much couldn't think about anything else.

She pulled me over to the mattress by the end wall, and the entire time her mouth was so warm and the blood was pounding in my ears and I couldn't get my breath. I couldn't think beyond the

fact that Mac, who I was totally crazy about, had her tongue in my mouth, doing things that I'd only imagined her doing but never really thought she ever would.

She moved her hands slowly over my back under my shirt, and everywhere she touched my skin, it felt like her fingers were still there when she moved them. I pulled her even tighter to me with one hand, and slid the other into her hair. Even though I'd kissed a bunch of girls, it was like I'd never kissed anyone before.

We sank down onto the mattress on our knees like some cheesy movie love scene. Mac's hand came around my body, and she started pulling down the zipper of my hoodie, and somewhere in the back of my mind I knew where she was going, and oh shit, did I want to go there. I'd dreamed of going there from pretty much the first time I saw her,

and it took willpower I didn't know I even had to pull my mouth off of hers, swallow a couple of times and whisper hoarsely, "Are you sure?"

She smiled at me. The most beautiful smile I ever remember seeing, and all she said was, "Yes."

I studied her face for a moment, and I couldn't see anything that made me think that she didn't want to, or that she was afraid or even that deep down inside she thought I was gross. Of course, I didn't want to see that either.

"I have a…you know," I mumbled, feeling my face get hot. I didn't want her to think I was the kind of guy who carried protection everywhere because I was always looking for someone to jump.

She grabbed the neck of my shirt and pulled me toward her. I dropped my mouth back onto hers, and I just let go and fell into the feeling of being

with Mac, of loving Mac the way I'd been dreaming of for the past six months.

Have you ever thought about something so much that when it happened, it just wasn't as good, it just couldn't be, because of how perfect you'd made it in your mind?

This wasn't like that. It was everything I'd always thought about and better. It wasn't like I'd never done *it* before, but this was special, and I didn't mean to, but I even whispered, "I love you, Mac," softly against her hair, because I needed to do that.

After, we lay wrapped up in the blankets with Mac in my arms, her head on my chest. Her hair smelled like flowers. I was almost afraid to say anything in case somehow it all turned out to be a mistake.

"Hey, Danny Boy, remember that first day we talked, on the merry-go-round in the park? Back then, I didn't

know you had chest hair and muscles," Mac said, tracing small, slow circles on my chest.

How many times had I gone over that day in my mind? I'd been walking home after school. I always cut through the park because it was faster than taking the long way around on the sidewalk. There had been no one around except for Mac, who was sitting on the edge of the merry-go-round.

I saw her and I had wanted to talk to her. I just wasn't sure if I should. So I was walking along, sort of staring at my feet, trying to decide what to do, and I was almost past her when she called out, "Hey, you're in my home-room, aren't you?"

I stopped and looked at her. "Yeah," I said. "I'm Daniel, middle of the row by the window." As soon as the words were out, I knew how dumb they sounded. Mac just kind of shrugged and said,

"I'm Mac, stuck in the front row because I'm the new kid." Then she had grinned, and wow, I couldn't say anything at all, dumb or otherwise. There was pretty much no blood left in my brain.

"Mac, why do you always call me Danny Boy?" I asked now, concentrating on the feeling of her finger, which was already starting to make me feel crazy all over again.

She didn't answer for so long that I thought she wasn't going to. Then finally she said, "It's an old song my grandmother liked. Sometimes she'd sing it to me."

"Oh," I said, mostly because I didn't know what else to say.

I closed my eyes for a minute just to let myself enjoy the feeling of her hand moving on my skin. When I woke up, Mac was gone.

Chapter Five

I jerked upright and looked around.
It was almost dark. I called Mac's name
a couple of times, but she didn't answer
me. I yanked on my pants and went
barefoot across the hall to the other
slanted-roof bedroom. She wasn't there.
I went down the stairs, still calling for
her. I walked all around the downstairs.
She wasn't anywhere in the house.

It wasn't until I went back up to the room to put on the rest of my clothes that I saw the words written on the wall above the air mattress. They hadn't been there before. I was sure of that. Just two words.

Danny Boy.

I didn't know what it meant. Was she sorry we'd done it? Was she happy? Were we still friends? Were we something else?

I pulled on the rest of my things and took one last look at that ceiling in the dim light, full of Mac's words, full of Mac's dreams. It was just wrong that it was going to be destroyed in the morning. And I wondered if I'd been wrong not to take pictures of as much as I could, even though she'd said she didn't want me to. It was too late now.

I let myself out of the back door of the little house, looked around to make

sure no one was watching, then sprinted across the torn-up lawn and pushed through the opening in the fence. Once I was away from the house, I pulled out my phone and tried Mac. All I got was her voice mail. For a second, I didn't know what to leave for a message. Finally I said, "Hey, uh, Mac, it's Daniel. Call me. Please."

Not very original.

So now what? I didn't feel like going home. I'd been walking more or less down the hill, and I realized that I wasn't that far from Frankie and Johnnie's. Frankie and Johnnie's was this retro diner, lots of neon, red vinyl and shiny chrome. Mac loved the place, and they probably had the best onion rings in the world, or at least in this podunkville part of it.

Thinking about the onion rings made me hungry, so I figured I'd stop in for an order and maybe Mac would call

while I was sitting there, or maybe she'd somehow already be there.

She wasn't.

Alex and Ren were sitting at a round table by the window. Alex's hair was purple again and spiked, which had to be Ren's doing. I got my order and went over to them. Alex was sitting sideways in his seat, drumming on the tabletop to some beat only he could hear. He did that sort of thing a lot. Bass players are kind of out there. At least all the ones I've met.

"Hey," I said, snagging a chair from the next table with my foot and dragging it over so I could sit down.

"Mac's not here, Daniel," Ren said, pulling her hands back through her thick blond hair and then letting it fall to her shoulders like some kind of shampoo commercial.

"Kinda noticed that," I said around a mouthful of onion and crispy, greasy deep-fried batter.

"Yeah, well, don't bug her, okay?" Ren said, dipping what looked like a cold French fry into a blob of mayonnaise on her plate and stuffing it in her mouth.

Ren and Alex were more Mac's friends than mine. The three of them had met in detention. I'd never been sent to detention, and Ren sometimes acted like that was a moral failure on my part.

"What's it to you?" I said, dunking half an onion ring into ketchup, because who eats fries or onion rings with mayonnaise anyway?

"After last night, she just needs to be by herself for a while."

"What happened last night?" The only thing I knew that had been going on the night before had been the school dance, and I knew Mac would never go to one of those. She thought school dances were lame. Besides, she'd already told me

she'd been in the music room finishing her comp project.

Ren looked at me like I was stupid or something. Of course, compared to her, I was. Compared to her, everyone was dumb as dirt. Ren had an IQ that made her pretty much smarter than everyone—for sure smarter than every teacher in school, plus the principal. (Okay, so you didn't have to be a genius to be smarter than Mr. Kenner.)

Teachers were always on Ren's case because she "didn't apply herself." That's school talk for she did dick-all in class. Ren figured, what was the point? Everyone went on to the next grade every year—holding someone back was too damaging to our fragile self-esteem. So she decided what was the point of actually studying? First of all, she pretty much knew everything anyway. If she read a book, what she read was in her head forever. And how smart

was it to do homework for marks that you didn't need?

It made sense to me, and I guess it did to Ren's parents too, because it didn't matter how many times they were called in to the school, nothing ever changed.

Ren shook her head and made a face. "You didn't hear, did you?"

"Hear what?" I asked, before taking a long drink from my Coke.

She looked at Alex, and he shrugged.

"There was a dance last night," she said.

"Yeah, I did hear about that."

"You know Gavin Healey?" she asked, dunking another cold French fry in mayo and eating it. For some reason, watching her made me think of a bird eating a worm.

"Mr. Hot-Shot-I'm-Gonna-Play-in-the-NHL? He's in my math class. He's a jerk." I stuffed another onion ring in my mouth, chewed and swallowed.

"What does Gavin have to do with the school dance and Mac?"

"Mac had a date with Gavin last night."

Chapter Six

I almost choked on my drink. I coughed, leaning over the table trying to get my breath, reaching blindly for a napkin to wipe my face. "You have lost your mind," I said to Ren. "In the first place, Mac wouldn't be caught dead at a school dance, and there's no way she'd ever go out with an asshole like Gavin Healey. No way!"

"You don't know her as well as you think you do," Ren said, and there was something—pity, no, something else, sadness maybe—in her blue eyes.

"Yeah, well, I know Mac well enough to know that she would never be interested in Gavin Healey." *How could she be*, I thought, *after what we'd just done? That meant something. It had to, didn't it?*

"It wasn't really a date," Ren said. She took a deep breath and let it out. "Mac didn't know that. It was just a big stupid setup between Gavin and his asshole friends on the hockey team. They wanted to make Mac look like a loser. They thought it was funny."

"No way. Shit! No."

Alex fished in the pocket of his jeans, got his phone out and pulled up something on the screen. He leaned forward, holding the phone out to me. "Sorry, man," he said.

It was a picture someone had emailed him, clearly taken at the dance the night before. In the background, I could see Gavin licking some girl's face, with his hand on her ass. It wasn't Mac.

That's because the rest of the picture was Mac, her face mostly, and the look on it made my chest ache. There was so much pain on her face, so much hurt.

I turned my head away and stared out the window. My hands were clenched into tight fists, and I wished Gavin were there so I could pound him into a pile of hamburger.

"Did you know Mac was helping Gavin with math?" Ren asked, leaning forward with her elbows on the table.

"No," I said.

Ren snapped the end of her knife with her thumb and finger and started it spinning. "Me neither. And mostly I think it was just Mac doing his work for him."

I pushed the plate of half-eaten onion rings away. I wasn't hungry anymore. "Why would she do something like that?" I asked.

The helping with math part, I got. Mac was a math genius. But doing Gavin Healey's assignments? Doing anyone's assignments? That wasn't her.

"She liked Gavin," Ren said. "That's why."

I shook my head. It still didn't make sense.

"C'mon, you didn't think she liked you or something?"

"No," I said, feeling my cheeks start to burn.

Ren did that hands-through-her-hair thing again, and I caught the sparkle of green glass in her ears. My arm shot across the table and grabbed her wrist. "Where did you get those earrings?" I said.

Alex straightened up in his seat, and it crossed my mind that he was twice as big as I was and, if he wanted to, he could pretty much pick me up and break me into little pieces. I let go of Ren and held up my hand so they both knew I didn't mean anything by grabbing her in the first place.

"Hey, I'm sorry," I said. I took a deep breath and let it out slowly. Then I asked the question again. "Where did you get those earrings?"

Her hand touched the dangly glass and metal, and she smiled, sort of. "Mac gave them to me."

I didn't know what to do with my hands, and the urge to grab her again was strong. "When?" I said.

"A little while ago," Ren said, sliding her chair back. Away from me?

"Mac was here?"

"Yeah."

I cleared my throat. "Those are her favorite earrings."

They were just two loops of copper wire with three rows of tiny glass beads strung across the loop—a couple of tiny abacuses. They'd been a present from Mac's grandmother the last Christmas she'd been alive. They were the only earrings she ever wore. She'd been wearing them when we were...together at the house. They'd sparkled in the fading light when she'd lifted her head to look at me and I'd thought my heart was going to beat its way out of my chest.

"She said she didn't want them anymore and she knew I'd always liked them, so she asked if I wanted them, and I said yes."

"You didn't think that was weird?" I asked.

"No," Ren said, and her eyes kind of slid off my face. "When she wants them again, I'll just give them back to her."

Ren was a crappy liar.

Chapter Seven

"You think she's going to take off again, don't you? Did she tell you that?" I hadn't eaten any more onion rings, so why did I have this lump in my throat that I couldn't seem to swallow down?

Ren looked away and didn't answer.

The thing was, when life got too hard for Mac, she ran. I knew she'd run away right after her grandmother died,

when she had to switch to Riverview, and then she'd taken off a couple of months ago after some big blowup with her uncle. I wondered if that was when he'd told her he was going to sell the little green house.

I didn't know where she'd gone or what she'd done those two times before. She was just gone, and everyone— Mr. Kenner, Mrs. Robinson—kept asking, had she called us, had she said anything? And then three or four days later she was back like nothing had happened. When I asked her where she'd gone, she just shrugged.

The last time, before she took off, she'd given Ren her favorite purple scarf, and she'd given me this funny little windup chicken that did the bird dance. It was like she didn't want us to forget her in case she didn't come back, but of course she had.

Now Mac had given Ren those earrings. That had to mean she was planning on taking off again, except she hadn't given anything to me yet. Then it hit me that she kind of had.

I still couldn't swallow whatever was caught in my throat. "What did she say, Ren?" I said.

"She didn't say anything. She just gave me the earrings."

"She's taking off again. I know she is." I pulled a hand over my face.

"You don't know that," Ren said. "And anyway, you can't say anything to anybody. Just let Mac work things out in her own way. She needs some time by herself, that's all."

"Running away is stupid," I said. "It doesn't fix anything."

"Yeah, well, that's Mac's business, not yours," Ren said. "Don't go all weird about stuff, like Shannon did."

Shannon.

She was Mac's friend for a little while, another math genius who hated gym class like Mac did, which meant they were always the last two people changing in the locker room. She saw some scars and cuts on Mac's arm and went to Mrs. Robinson, who is probably the world's worst guidance counselor. She overreacts to everything.

There was a whole lot of drama. We all got called into Mrs. Robinson's office one at a time so she could ask us if we'd ever seen Mac hurt herself or if we thought she was depressed. (That would be *no* and *no*.) And Mrs. Robinson got to give her I'm-here-for-you speech probably ten times—like anyone was going to take her up on that.

Finally Mac had to admit that she'd gotten the cuts on her arm when she was trying to wreck some of the equipment the city was using to take

down the merry-go-round at the park—the same one where we'd gotten to be friends. Mac loved that merry-go-round. I think it had something to do with her grandmother.

She hadn't actually damaged anything, but she'd tried to, which was almost as bad. She got detention for a month, and The Asshole grounded her—not that that worked for long—and she had to spend two weekends picking up garbage in the park.

She never spoke to Shannon again. It was like Shannon was dead. Mac just looked right through her and froze her out.

"I'm not that stupid," I said. I wasn't going to do anything that would make Mac start acting like I didn't exist.

"So you won't say anything?" Ren asked. "C'mon, you know how Mac is. Once she figures stuff out, she'll come back. She always does."

"I'm not going to say anything. Give it a rest, Ren," I said. I shoved my chair back and got to my feet. There was a buzzing sound in my ears like a hive of bees had somehow gotten inside my head. "I gotta go," I said. Ren said something else, but I couldn't hear what it was.

Chapter Eight

Outside, I just started walking fast, hands jammed in my pockets. I didn't know where I was going, and I didn't care. I just needed to get away from Ren and Alex.

Mac liked Gavin Healey. Was that why she'd had sex with me? Out of spite because Gavin made her look stupid in front of most of the school? Or was it her gift to me because she was taking

off again? Last time I got a dancing chicken, so this time I got laid?

So why did she take me to the house? Why did she show me her room and that ceiling if it didn't mean anything?

I needed to talk to Mac. I pulled out my phone and tried her again. I got voice mail. Again.

"It's Daniel. Please call me," I said.

Okay, she wasn't answering her phone, so I'd just find her and ask her what the hell was going on. Except I didn't know where to look. When we weren't at school, or in the music room or with Ren and Alex, I didn't know what Mac did. I realized I didn't know where she lived. I didn't even know The Asshole's real name.

I leaned against a telephone pole. I was so lame. How could I say I was Mac's friend? I didn't really know her at all. Her having sex with me was pretty much the same as her giving Ren a pair

of earrings. It didn't mean anything beyond that she liked to give people presents before she took off in case she decided not to come back.

The onion rings lay like a greasy lump in my stomach. I thought about going home, but I didn't really want to talk to my mother. She'd know something wasn't right. She had this weird mother thing where she could tell something was wrong with me, no matter how hard I tried to hide it. It was almost like she could see inside my head.

What would I say to her? "Hey, Mom, I slept with this girl I'm crazy about, in this old house that's about to be torn down, but it turns out the whole thing didn't mean squat because she's taking off, and she decided sleeping with me was a better goodbye present than a windup chicken."

No, that wouldn't freak her out or anything.

I looked around and realized that I wasn't that far from the school. I figured I might as well walk over there and see if Mr. Hanson was around so maybe I could at least get into the music room and work on my composition project.

What were the chances he'd be at the school on a Saturday night? Pretty good, actually. Mr. Hanson's love life seemed to be about as lame as mine was.

I could see the lights on in the music room as I came around the side of the old stone building. Mr. Hanson was at the piano. No one else seemed to be around. How big a loser was I?

I stood there in the darkness thinking maybe I should go somewhere else. Do something else. Yeah, great idea, except I didn't have anything else to do or anywhere else to go.

I banged on the window. Mr. Hanson looked up, smiled when he saw me and

gestured for me to come around to the end door so he could let me in.

"Hi, Daniel," he said.

"Hi, Mr. Hanson," I said, mostly faking a smile. My voice sounded kind of hoarse, and I coughed to clear it. "Is it okay if I work on my project?"

"Sure," he said. "I'm going to be here for probably another forty-five minutes." He didn't ask me why I had nothing better to do than hang out at school on a Saturday night. Maybe he figured if he asked me, I might ask him.

I wondered sometimes why he hung out in the music department so much after school hours. Didn't he have a girlfriend? He wasn't bad-looking for a guy his age. He was tall. He wasn't fat. He had all his original hair. It was half gray, but he didn't wear it in some kind of dorky ponytail in the back or anything.

Maybe he was thinking the same think about me, wondering why I didn't have a girlfriend. I wasn't ugly, and I was fairly tall. Okay, so I didn't have a lot of muscles, but I wasn't some skinny geek boy either. And I took a shower every day and put on clean clothes. My mother said when I got a bit older, girls would be all over me. What else was she supposed to say? She was my mother.

I got my folder from the back of the room and plugged a set of headphones into my favorite keyboard. Then I put my music on the stand, except there really wasn't much music, because I'd been stuck on this dumb assignment for more than a week.

I wanted to write a song for Mac. Stupid, I know. But I couldn't make it sound right, and the harder I tried, the more it just sucked. I closed my eyes and tried to remember what it had felt like when she kissed me. No girl had

ever had a mouth so soft and warm. I thought about my skin next to hers, and suddenly my fingers were moving over the keys.

I found a pencil, and for the next forty-five minutes I played and transcribed and Mac's song came to life. I pulled off the headphones just as Mr. Hanson came over to me.

"Progress?" he asked.

I nodded. "Yeah."

"Sorry I have to kick you out," he said.

"It's okay." I stuffed the music in my folder before he could look at what I'd done. I wasn't ready to show it to anyone yet. "I'm pretty much finished."

I put my folder back in my slot and hung the headphones inside the cupboard. Mr. Hanson pulled on his jacket, grabbed his backpack and carefully picked up something wrapped in a green plastic bag. "Can you hold this while I lock up?" he asked, holding out the bag.

"Sure," I said.

"Don't drop it," he said lightly, though there was an edge of seriousness to his voice.

"What is this? Our final exam?" I asked as he took out his keys.

He looked at me over his shoulder and grinned. "No, something way more valuable than that. Long John Baldry's 1971 album, *It Ain't Easy*—the original, not the reissue, and vinyl, not CD."

I almost dropped the record. It was a good thing it was dark and he couldn't see my face, because he would have known something was up. "Where, uh, where did you get it?" I asked, and I was surprised at how normal my voice sounded, because I didn't feel normal at all. I already knew what he was going to say.

Chapter Nine

"Your friend Mac gave it to me. I guess she found it in some old things that had belonged to her grandmother. She knew how much I like bluesmen like Baldry, so she asked if I wanted it. It didn't mean anything to her."

I was glad to hand the album back to him, because my hands were shaking so badly it would have ended up on

the parking lot pavement in another minute.

"I, uh, I gotta go," I said.

"Good night, Daniel," he said. "See you Monday."

I walked away from him across the parking lot in long strides and then blindly down the street until I was out of sight of the school. Then I stopped and sat on the curb.

I couldn't breathe, and every part of me was shaking—my hands, my arms, my legs. My teeth would have been banging together if I hadn't been biting on my tongue so hard I could taste blood.

Mac had gotten that album from her grandmother. She had a whole collection of them, old stuff like Long John Baldry. She liked the pops and hisses and scratches those old records made. Maybe because she'd listened to so many of them with her grandmother.

But that Baldry album was her treasure. Mac's grandmother was a huge fan. The album had been hers, and I knew that the liner inside had Long John Baldry's signature. Mac would never give that away.

It meant nothing to her? No way. It meant everything.

I pulled both hands back through my hair. I knew Mac liked Mr. Hanson, even though she said all teachers were lame. Giving him the album was like giving Ren her earrings and me...well, herself. She was going to run again because of Gavin and because her grandmother's house was going to get torn down. Except I was starting to think that this time she wasn't going to come back.

I pulled out my phone and punched in Mac's number, and the whole time all I was saying in my head was, "Pleaseanswer, pleaseanswer, pleaseanswer," and she didn't.

And I didn't know what to say, what message to leave on her voice mail. Please don't run away again because I love you? I'd already said "I love you" to Mac, and I'd noticed that she hadn't said it back.

I don't know how long I was there sitting on the edge of the curb, shaking. Finally I decided I should move or someone was going to see me and think I was stoned or something and call the cops.

So I got up and started walking again, and I guess my feet were on some kind of autopilot, because I was almost home before I noticed which direction I was going in.

I let myself in the back door and stood in the darkness in the kitchen for a minute, listening, trying to guess where my mother was. My dad was on a business trip to Los Angeles. While I was standing there, Mom came into

the room, saw me standing there and gave a little shriek.

"It's just me, Mom," I said, holding up a hand.

She put her own hand flat on her chest, shaking her head. "What are you doing standing in the middle of the kitchen in the dark?" she said. "If you were trying to scare me to death, it didn't work, but it was close."

"I'm sorry," I said. "I was just thinking."

She padded over to the cupboard and took down a bag of dill pickle chips from the shelf. I could see the bag was already half gone and I hadn't had any. She bought baked chips because they were healthier, but then she ate them all, which didn't seem that healthy to me.

"So what were you thinking about?" Mom asked, tipping her head on one side to look up at me. My mother

was short, which didn't mean she didn't know about twenty-seven different ways to put you down on your knees if you gave her any trouble. She had four big brothers.

"Were you thinking about why we're all here on this planet, or were you trying to decide whether you wanted frozen pizza or the last piece of cake?"

She always asked questions like that. My friends either thought my mother was deeply weird, or they kind of had a thing for her, mostly the last part.

I shrugged and hoped it looked casual so maybe just this once she wouldn't notice anything off about me. "I was just, you know, thinking about school and stuff."

She popped another chip in her mouth and held out the bag to me. I took a handful even though I wasn't that crazy about dill pickle chips.

"What's wrong?" she asked in the same tone she'd used when she'd asked me if I was trying to decide between frozen pizza and leftover cake.

For a second, I thought about telling her that I'd slept with Mac and it was wonderful, but after, she'd just disappeared and I couldn't find her, and she was giving presents to her friends just the way she had the last time she ran away, except I was afraid that this time she wouldn't come back in a few days.

What kind of loser tells his mother stuff like that? So instead I just said, "Nothing."

Her eyebrows went up, but she ate another chip before she said anything. "You don't lie very well, Daniel."

"I'm not lying," I said, shifting from one foot to the other.

She set the bag on the counter and leaned back against the cupboard.

"I can't help you if I don't know what the problem is," she said softly.

"Nothing's wrong," I said again, looking up at the ceiling and shaking my head. "So there isn't anything to help me with."

Mom stared at me for a long moment, and it was hard not to move or at least look away, but I didn't.

"Okay," she said. She picked up the bag of chips again and pushed past me.

Chapter Ten

Once she was gone, I slumped against the counter and folded both arms over my head. How could I tell her what was going on? If I did, she'd be calling the school and Mac's uncle and maybe even the police, and Mac wouldn't be able to take off, if she hadn't already, but she'd never speak to me again. It wasn't like I was six and I could just go running

to my mommy. That's not how the world worked.

"No, it's not okay," my mother's voice said then.

I lifted my head and opened my eyes. I hadn't even heard her come back into the room.

She was standing in the doorway. "Something's wrong, Daniel," she said, "and I'm not going to pretend I don't know that." She sighed. "Please talk to me."

I shook my head. "Just leave me alone, Mom."

"Can't do that, kiddo."

"There's nothing you can do." And she couldn't. Mac wasn't answering her phone, and I didn't know where she was or even where to start looking for her. I didn't know where she'd taken off to the last two times she'd left.

And how pissed would she be if I was wrong? Maybe she wasn't going to run off. People got tired of stuff and

gave it away all the time. I had an old bike in our garage I was going to give away, and that didn't mean I was going to leave home.

"You can't help," I said.

Mom pushed a piece of hair back behind her ear. "I can do all kinds of things," she said.

I was starting to get angry, which felt a lot better than the cold lump of fear that had been sitting like a rock in my stomach ever since I'd left the school. "Really?" I said. I sounded kind of snarky. "What? You got some kind of superpowers?"

The only thing that gave away that she was pissed was the way her jaw tightened. I knew she was clenching her teeth together. "I'm going to make a cup of coffee," she said. "You're going up to sit in your room."

I pushed away from the counter. "You're not sending me to my room like I'm a little kid or something."

"Then stop acting like you're a little kid." She pulled herself up to her full height of five foot nothing. I was taller, but that didn't make a difference to her.

"Daniel, something is clearly, clearly wrong. All I'm trying to do is help you. I'm not trying to tell you how to run your life, I'm not even trying to tell you what to do, because I don't know what the heck the problem is. I just want to help."

She put her hand on my arm, and I twisted away from her. It struck me that all the time I'd spent here in the kitchen talking to her had just been time wasted when I could have been looking for Mac. Suddenly I couldn't stand there one more second. I had to get out. I had to look for Mac.

I just turned and walked away from Mom toward the back door.

"Where are you going?" she said. She came behind me and grabbed the

back of my sweatshirt, knocking me off balance for a moment.

I didn't have time for her. I pulled both arms out of the shirt and kept going.

"Daniel!" she called.

"Leave me alone," I shouted. I never yelled at her, but I had to get away and find Mac. I ran across the driveway. I was out of breath, and my nose was running. I looked all around, and I knew there was no way I'd be able to get away with the car, but there was that old bicycle I'd brought up from the basement to give away. I swiped a hand across my face, grabbed the bike and started pedaling down the driveway. My mother ran after me but couldn't catch me. I heard her yell my name a couple of times, but I didn't answer. I just pedaled like crazy and I didn't look back.

Chapter Eleven

I don't know how far I went before I stopped. My chest burned, and it felt like it was packed full of sand. I hung over the handlebars, wheezing until I got my breath.

Okay. Okay, so what did I do now? I figured there was pretty much no chance that Mac was going to answer her phone, but I tried her again anyway

and like all the times before I got her voice mail. I didn't leave a message this time either. What would I say anyway? *Hey, Mac, it's Daniel and you're scaring the crap out of me because I'm afraid you're taking off and never coming back so call me and tell me I'm crazy. Okay?*

The only thing I could think of was to find her. Maybe she wasn't gone yet. Maybe somebody knew where she was heading. The only place I could think of to start was with the last two people that I knew had seen Mac. Ren and Alex.

It was Saturday night, and I knew where they had to be, where they always were. At the late movie at the Empire. Ren had a thing for old, old movies, and Alex had a thing for Ren, so that's what they did on Saturday nights. They went to the Empire. One week they'd show weepy romantic films, and the next it would be some teenagers-getting-chopped-up-with-an-ax marathon.

I took off in the direction of the old theater. The tires were soft and I hadn't been on a bike in a while, so I was kind of all over the place on the pavement. A car rolled by me and the driver yelled, "Get off the road asshole," out the side window.

My hands were shaking so bad, I stopped at the next intersection. I thought for a second I was going to puke on the street. Was this stupid? Was I going to find Mac and she'd be okay and just laugh at me? Right now I'd take that. Right now that would sound so good.

I made it the rest of the way to the Empire. Ren and Alex were in the middle of the line, and I was happy that I didn't have to buy a ticket and try to have this conversation inside.

I walked up to them and touched Ren on the shoulder. I could see Mac's green beaded earring caught in Ren's hair like

a little green light, and somehow that gave me courage.

"Do you know where Mac's going?" I said.

Ren turned to look at me. "Hey, Daniel," she said.

Alex was in front of her, and he swung around at the same time, and for the second time that night I thought about how big he was and how easily he could and probably would pound me into sand in a minute. He was a couple of inches taller for sure, and even his muscles had muscles.

Then Mac's earring winked at me again and I pushed the thought away. "Look, I won't tell her you told me," I said, hating how desperate I sounded. "I just really need to talk to her."

Ren sighed and shook her hair back from her face. "Daniel, you just have to leave Mac alone for now."

"I only want to talk to her for a minute, just a minute," I said. "Please, Ren."

"I don't know where she is," she said. "And I wouldn't tell you if I did." She shrugged and turned away from me.

I lost it. I grabbed her shoulder and pulled her back around to face me, knowing that in about five seconds Alex was going to have me flat on the sidewalk using my head for a punching bag. "Just tell me where she is," I said, my face pressed close to Ren's.

A second later, Alex was shoving me back against the wall of the old movie theater. My head banged against the bricks, and explosions of light went off behind my eyelids.

Alex had one huge hand on my chest and the other pressed against my face so I could only breathe through one corner of my mouth. He caught a fistful of hair and was about to smash my head against

the wall again when an air horn went off against his right ear.

His arm went up over the side of his head. He took a couple of staggering steps backward and made a sound like there was something stuck in his throat and he was about to puke it out. My mother was standing there with the air horn in her hand.

Chapter Twelve

I straightened up, and she shot me a look. "You all right?" she asked. I gave a small nod, which set the fireworks off again. I saw her free hand move as though she was going to reach up and check the back of my head, but something in my face stopped her. It was bad enough that I'd just had my butt saved by my mother.

Mom looked from Alex, who I knew was really going to kill me the next time he saw me, to Ren. Her gaze settled on Ren. "Daniel asked you a question," she said. There was no anger in her voice. She could have been Mrs. Henderson asking us to solve $3x + y$.

Ren looked back at my mom. She wasn't scared. That was the thing about being the smartest person in the room all the time—you didn't worry about other people. She shrugged. "You're not my mother," she said. "I don't have to talk to you. And I'm not." She went back to the line—a couple of people in it were staring at us—and Alex followed her, smacking the palm of one hand with his other fist and glaring at me. I tried not to think about how the next time he did that with his fist, it would probably be my face on the other end.

I started after Ren, and Mom's arm shot out. "She isn't going to tell you anything," she said.

I opened my mouth to argue, but I knew she was right. I watched Ren and Alex buy their tickets and go inside. Neither one of them looked back even once.

"Car's over there," Mom said, pointing.

I walked across the street with her—what the hell else could I do?—and got in the passenger side. Mom put the air horn on the backseat. "Let me see your head," she said. When I hesitated, she tipped her own head toward the backseat. "Don't make me use that again."

I leaned forward, and she ran her fingers over my scalp. I winced when she touched the spot where I'd made contact with the wall.

She laid her hand against the side of my face for a moment and then sat back

in her seat. "There's no blood," she said. "Can you see okay?"

"Yeah, you always have two heads, right?"

"You're so funny," she said. "But you need to be checked out by a doctor."

"Jeez, Mom," I said. "I just scraped my head against the wall. Swear to God. Alex was about to beat my head into spaghetti, but he didn't get the chance." I looked over my shoulder into the backseat. "Where did you get that thing anyway?"

"Hockey game," she said.

"You took an air horn to a hockey game?"

The same piece of hair kept falling into her face, and she tucked it back behind her ear again. "No. The guy sitting behind me took it to the game. I just convinced him it was a better idea to give it to me."

Maybe there was stuff about me that my mother didn't know, but it seemed like there was stuff I didn't know about her either.

"Are you going to tell me what's going on?" Mom asked. "You're looking for someone named Mac?"

I stared out the windshield for a minute. "Uh-huh," I finally said.

"And she's friends with those two?"

I pushed my hair back off my face. "Ren and Alex. Yeah."

"Wren? Like the bird?"

I shook my head. It still hurt, but I didn't want Mom to see that, or I'd be on my way to the emergency room. "No, R-E-N. It's short for Renata."

"Who's Mac and why are you looking for her?"

The minute she said the words, I could feel the lump pressing again in my stomach. I couldn't look at her. I stared

out the side window. If I said the words, would it make them true?

She waited, and the silence stretched between us, like a rubber band pulling tighter and tighter and thinner and thinner.

And then I said it. "She's my friend, and I think she's going to kill herself." Because that's what I was really afraid of, that's what had been buzzing in the back of my head since I'd seen Mr. Hanson with that old record album. Not that Mac was going to run off from this life and never come back, but that she was going to end her life, forever, because it was one thing to give stuff to her friends, but giving that album to a teacher, *a teacher*, that was different.

I couldn't help thinking that maybe Shannon had been right about Mac hurting herself. Maybe the rest of us had been wrong. Maybe Mac had lied.

Maybe things seemed a lot darker to her than I knew.

Mom sucked in a breath. She laid her hand on mine, and I felt her warmth sink into me. "Why do you think that?" she asked.

Chapter Thirteen

I swallowed, trying to get rid of the sour, burning taste at the back of my throat, but I couldn't.

I told Mom everything then, even about sex with Mac. I told her about Mac's grandmother, about the little green house, about the ceiling covered with Mac's poetry and songs. I told her about Shannon, how she'd tried to help

Mac and how Mac—and the rest of us—had treated her like a fink.

I told her about Mac running away the two other times that I knew about, and how she'd given me the dancing chicken the last time, and that this time she'd given Ren her earrings and Mr. Hanson her Baldry album. She already knew what Mac had given me. I even told her what had happened at the dance.

"It's different this time," I said. "This time she didn't just give people presents, she gave away the things that mattered to her the most."

"Mac lives with her uncle?" Mom asked.

I nodded. "I don't know where he lives and I don't know his name. Mac just calls him The Asshole."

"That's okay," she said, pulling out her phone.

"What are you doing?" I said.

"I'm calling Jeff Hanson, your music teacher. We need to find out if Mac is home."

"You think I'm right," I said. I could hardly get out the words.

"I think we need to know," she said.

I don't know if there is a God or not. My parents went to church, and a few times a year I went with them, mostly because it made my mom happy. But now, while she talked to Mr. Hanson, I prayed. I looked up at the stars through the car windshield and I prayed that Mac was home with The Asshole and his wife and that tomorrow she'd be pissed as hell at me because I freaked.

Finally Mom snapped her phone shut. "He's going to call me back," she said. She put her hand on top of mine again. "Tell me about Mac," she said.

I wasn't really sure what to say. I told her about the lyrics Mac wrote, how they were poetry, really. I told her how Mac's

face looked when she was working on a math problem. I told her about the first day she'd showed up in our class and how I'd been walking home through the park after school and found Mac at the old merry-go-round. I told how when Mac smiled at me, I sometimes couldn't breathe.

Mom's phone rang then, and as she answered I found myself making wild promises to God in my head. When she closed the phone and looked at me, I knew they hadn't worked.

"I'm sorry," Mom said. "She's not home."

I dropped my head to my chest, both arms folded over it like I was in a cocoon. "Mac's uncle—his name is Devin McCauley—and Mr. Hanson are on their way over to Mac's grandmother's house, to see if she's there. Mrs. Robinson is calling her other friends."

"She doesn't have any other friends," I snapped, my voice partly muffled against my chest. "She has me and Ren and Alex. That's it."

For a moment, Mom's hand stayed on mine, warm and steady. Then she reached up and pulled my arms away from my head. "Okay then," she said, "you're it. You're just going to have to figure out where she is."

"I don't know," I shouted. My nose was running again, and I wiped it with my sleeve. My cheeks were wet. I didn't even know I was crying. "She already went to all of her favorite places—the park, her grandmother's house, Frankie and Johnnie's, the music room at school."

And then I knew.

"What?" Mom said. She must have seen something in my face.

I swiped my sleeve across my face again. "The merry-go-round, you know,

the one I told you about where I saw Mac that first day. She loved that thing. When they took it out, she tried to get a petition going to bring it back. Didn't work."

"The city was worried about liability," Mom said, more to herself than me.

"When we were at the house earlier, she said something about the day we met at the merry-go-round." I was shaking. I looked at Mom. "She's there. Not at the park, I mean wherever they took it. She's there."

Mom was already pulling out her phone. "First we have to find out where *there* is."

"Who are you calling?"

"Someone from church who works for the planning department."

"It's almost midnight," I said.

She put the phone to her ear and reached into the backseat with her other hand to grab the sweatshirt I'd left

in the kitchen. "Good," she said. "That means he'll probably be home."

My hands were shaking so bad, I could barely get the shirt on and zippered. By the time I did, Mom was off the phone, starting the car and doing up her seatbelt all in one blur of motion.

"Buckle up," she said to me, and she put the car in gear and did a tight U-turn in the middle of the street.

"Where are we going?" I said.

"City garage." Her eyes were fixed on the road. At the corner she looked both ways and then ran the red light.

My thoughts were falling all over themselves. What if Mac was at the merry-go-round? What if she wasn't? What if we couldn't find her? What if… what if I was right and it was already too late? I closed my eyes and sent up one more prayer: *Please, God, let me be wrong.*

Chapter Fourteen

The car tires squealed as we whipped into the parking area of the city garage. Mom shot across the pavement, stopping with a spray of gravel, nose in the far corner of the lot.

The fenced storage space was down an embankment. Mom slammed the car into park and was out the door before I even had my seatbelt off. We half slid,

half fell down the hill. I looked at my watch. I saw that it was almost midnight. Almost tomorrow.

What had Mac said? Tomorrow everything would be gone. Did she mean herself too?

I looked at the fence in front of me. "Boost me up," I said.

Mom laced her fingers together, and I put my foot on her hands. She was stronger than she looked. She grunted, pushing up with both arms, and I managed to grab the top metal edge of the fence. I reached one arm down, and she pulled herself up.

"Go," she said. "I'm right behind you."

I swung myself over and jumped, landing on the other side. The whole space was full of crap, everything from bulldozer tires to old truck beds and broken park benches. It wasn't a garage. It was a dump.

I looked for the old merry-go-round, but I couldn't see it anywhere. There was a stack of three oversized tires, maybe four or five feet high, and I scrambled up on top of them and scanned the lot.

Where are you, Mac? was the only thought running through my head. Mom climbed down the fence, wiped her hands on her jeans and looked around.

And then I saw it. I jumped off the tires, and one leg twisted and almost gave way underneath me, but I managed to stay upright.

"Call nine-one-one," I yelled, and then I started to run. I didn't look to see if she was doing it or if she'd even heard me. I just ran. Chest heaving, arms pumping, legs flying, I weaved around piles of junk, keeping my eyes locked on that merry-go-round at the far end of the fenced lot. Everything else blurred out of focus.

My lungs were burning, I'd never moved so fast. I didn't know I could.

I banged against some jagged-edged metal thing. My shirt tore and I felt the metal slice my skin, but I kept running. Behind me I could hear my mother pounding over the pavement, running too, breathing hard and heavy.

My mouth hung open as I tried to suck in air, and then we moved into an open space and…Oh God, I saw Mac, I saw Mac hanging by a rope from the top bar of the old merry-go-round.

Hanging by her neck.

"No!" I screamed. I stumbled and almost went down, but somehow I got my legs working again. I tore across the broken pavement and threw myself at the bottom half of Mac's body, hugging her legs, pushing up to make the rope looser around her neck.

She was warm. She was warm.

Tears ran down my face. "Take her!" I shouted at my mother. "Take her! She's not dead."

Mom wrapped her arms around Mac's legs and lifted up to keep the pressure off the rope. She clenched her teeth, breathing hard, and I could see the veins in her neck pulsing against her skin.

I let go and reached for one of the side supports of the merry-go-round, stretching as far as I could to pull myself up onto the top bar. I lay on my stomach on the narrow metal pipe and tried to undo the rope. The knot was too tight and too complicated, no matter how hard I pulled at the rope. I couldn't get her loose.

No! I pounded my fist on the bar.

No! I wasn't going to let this happen.

I looked down at my mom holding on to Mac, holding her up with every bit of strength she had. I wiped my face against the torn sleeve of my shirt and somehow my brain started working again.

"Mom." My voice was rough. "Do you have your knife?"

Her stupid knife. My dad had bought it for her because she was the kind of person who cut everything into small pieces and hated to get her hands dirty.

She nodded. "In my pocket," she said, her voice strained from the effort of holding on to Mac. "But I can't let go of her."

The sleeve of my shirt where I'd caught it on that stupid metal thing was wet with blood, and my arm was shaking even when I wasn't trying to use it. If I jumped down, could I climb back up again?

I wrapped my legs around the pipe and with my good arm reached down for Mac, catching her under both armpits and taking some of her weight from Mom. I only took one quick look at Mom's blotchy red face. Her eyes

were closed and her face, like mine, was wet with tears.

"Throw it," I yelled.

Mom kept one arm around Mac's legs and fished the penknife out of her jeans pocket with the other.

I used every bit of strength I had to hold Mac up with my one arm even as her weight pulled at me, trying to take both of us down. Except I wasn't going, and I wasn't letting her go either. I didn't care if my arm ripped right off my body, I wasn't letting go.

Mom threw the knife up in the air. It sailed toward me, end over end, and I could see it clearly, even in the darkness, like it was moving in slow motion. Mom grabbed on to Mac again with both arms, and I leaned out and snatched the knife out of the air and by some miracle managed not to fall.

I pulled the knife open with my teeth, jammed the blade between the metal

pipe and the rope and started to cut, using both hands. My legs were knotted with cramps. There were shooting pains going up both of my arms, but I wasn't going to stop. I gritted my teeth and worked at the rope with the knife.

Sirens wailed in the distance, getting closer. The rope began to fray and split as the blade sliced at it.

I was almost through. I slung my arm around Mac again, sawing with my shaking left arm, and suddenly the rope let go and we had all of Mac's weight. It almost pulled me over.

My legs started to give way. I let the knife fall to the ground and grabbed Mac around her chest with my other arm and somehow, with Mom's help, got her down to the ground without dropping her.

Mom's legs buckled. Her face twisted with pain, but she didn't make a sound. She crawled across the ground

to Mac, put an ear to her chest, and then she straightened and started chest compressions.

I jumped down, and my left ankle turned in when I landed, so I fell sideways onto my butt. There were raw, red marks on my hands from pulling on the rope. The same red marks I could see around Mac's neck.

Mom kept her eyes fixed on Mac's chest. I shoved my hair back off my face and put my mouth over Mac's. Something from my first-aid class kicked in and I remembered to tilt her head and check inside her mouth. Then I just breathed for both of us and focused everything else on the sound of my mother's voice calmly counting beside me.

Chapter Fifteen

The sirens got louder, drowning out my mother's voice, drowning out everything but the sound of my heart, pounding in my ears.

And then it happened. Mac's body jerked. She made a kind of strangled sound and tried to suck in a breath.

I pulled back as Mom turned Mac partly onto her side. Her breathing was

ragged and slow, but she was breathing.

She. Was. Breathing.

And then the ambulance was at the fence, red lights swirling. I tried to get to my feet, but my ankle wouldn't work right. Mom reached over and pushed me back down. Then she stood up herself, took a few steps forward and raised her hands over her head, waving so the paramedics could see us. And all the time I could hear Mac behind me, working to pull in every breath.

Alive.

The paramedics ran across the lot and pushed past us. Mom helped me move off to the side, out of the way. One of the paramedics came over to us but I shook my head. "I'm all right," I said. "Just take care of her, please."

Mom noticed my arm for the first time. "Daniel, you're hurt," she said.

"Just let them fix Mac first, please," I said.

Wordlessly she pulled off her own sweatshirt and draped it over my shoulders, putting her arm around me at the same time. We stayed like that while the two men worked.

Finally, after what seemed like a long time, they lifted Mac onto a stretcher. Her eyes were open, and I struggled to get to my feet, ignoring the pain in my ankle. I wanted to tell her I was there. I wanted to tell her she'd be okay. I leaned over, laying my hand on the blue sheet they'd covered her with.

She looked up at me. "Why didn't you let me die?" she rasped, her voice raw and low. Then she turned her head away and closed her eyes, tears slipping out from under her lashes.

I stood there as they moved the stretcher across the uneven ground. There were two police officers walking toward us.

Mom got to her feet. She held on to my arm with one of hers, and I looked at her. "She hates me," I said dully. I wasn't so stunned that I didn't know this was what Mac had done to Shannon when she'd tried to warn us that Mac was hurting herself. What we'd all done, me and Ren and Alex. And I wished I had a time machine so I could go back and do it differently, and maybe Mac would never have gotten to this.

Mom's face was pale and dirty. Half her hair was hanging in her eyes. She hugged herself with her free arm. She'd done all this for Mac. She'd done this for me. Was it all for nothing?

Then she looked up at me and smiled. She gave me this huge beautiful smile that didn't make any sense. "Yeah, she hates you right now," she said, "but the thing is, she's here to hate you, isn't she?"

Then she wrapped both her arms around me, still smiling that shining smile, and I put my head on her shoulder and cried because Mac hated me.

And I cried because Mac was here.

She was still here.

Darlene Ryan is the author of *Responsible, Saving Grace* and *Five Minutes More*. She is at work on another teen novel.

orca soundings

The following is an excerpt from
another exciting Orca Soundings novel,
Viral by Alex Van Tol.

978-1-55469-411-2 $9.95 pb
978-1-55469-412-9 $16.95 lib

MIKE HAS FALLEN FOR HIS BEST FRIEND,

Lindsay. And he's pretty sure she feels the same
way, until a simple misunderstanding destroys
Lindsay's trust.

When Lindsay ends up in a compromising
situation, someone is filming the whole thing, and
the footage goes viral. Mike has to help Lindsay
in her time of greatest need.

Chapter one

You only get one chance. Ever heard that saying?

It's true. Especially with the important things in life. So when that one chance rolls around, you can't afford to screw it up.

Except, somehow, I did.

Things had been going so well between Lindsay and me. After years of just being friends, something had shifted in the way I felt about her. I didn't want to be just friends anymore. And I could kind of tell she didn't either. You know, from the way she looked at me. The way she talked to me. The way we suddenly felt shy with each other when we hadn't before. The way my heart kind of skipped a beat when her name came up on my phone.

It took me months, but I had finally worked up the courage to ask Lindsay out. I had it all planned: I was going to ask her at the year-end party at Sara's place.

On the night of the party, I was nervous as hell. Which is stupid, really, because it's what both of us wanted. But still, you want to do things right, you know?

So anyway, after a few beers everyone was down at the fire pit, and just

Lindsay and I were left sitting on the back deck. It was a cool night in late June. Pink clouds. Still air. The universe had even arranged some lightning flashing on the horizon. Perfect.

Lindsay was lounging on a chaise. I was hanging out on the double swing. She shivered a little. My cue.

"Want my hoodie?"

She smiled and shook her head. "I'm okay." But then she rubbed her arms. Cue number two.

I patted the seat beside me. "Come sit," I said. I held up a corner of the blanket that was draped over the swing back. I could easily have tossed it to her. But that wasn't the point. I wanted her close to me. I couldn't exactly ask her out if she was, like, ten feet away.

Sharing a swing with my best friend was something I would've done without thinking twice just a few months ago. We would have sat together under the

blanket and listened to the sounds of laughter drifting up from the fire pit below. Laughed at how drunk other people were. Made fun of teachers we didn't like.

But when it actually *means* something…it's different.

She shrugged. "Sure," she said. "It *is* getting chilly." She stood up. Stretched. God, how had I spent all these years not wanting her? She moved toward the swing. "Shove your butt over, Mikey." I grinned and she sat down beside me. Kicked off her sandals and brought her legs up under her—those long gymnastics-ripped legs of hers. I handed her some blanket and she tucked her feet underneath. She leaned into me. "This okay?"

My stomach did a flip-flop. "Yep." Definitely okay. I took a deep breath. "So," I began. But then I didn't know what else to say. My mind was blank.

Lindsay looked up at me. "Yeah?" The lightning forked a little bit closer. The storm was still too far away for us to hear any thunder. "So?"

"Yeah. That's, uh, that's some pretty great lightning, you know?" I sounded like an idiot.

She put her head on my shoulder. "It's totally great lightning, Mike," she agreed. I heard the smile in her voice.

I got a grip on myself and tried again. I was going to do this. "Yeah, so, um, I wanted to ask you something," I said. I lifted a strand of her hair and wrapped it around my fingers. So soft.

"Mm-hmm?" she asked. "What's that?" Her arm drifted across my stomach and rested there. She never used to do *that*. She hooked her thumb in one of my belt loops. I took another deep breath and let it out slow. Real slow.

"Yeah, so, I was wondering…" Another deep breath. A flash of lightning lit up the horizon. Another followed right on its heels. A puff of wind flipped up the corner of the blanket, exposing Lindsay's legs. Her amazing endless legs. She reached down absently and flicked it back into place. Snugged up tighter to me.

"You were wondering…?"

And suddenly I just…chickened out. "Yeah, I was wondering…do you, uh, do you want…another beer?" I finished lamely. As soon as the words left my mouth, I was furious with myself.

"No," I said, backpedaling. "I mean, never mind. Never mind the beer." I sucked in another breath. "I actually meant to ask you if—"

Right then, Aaron and Morgan crashed through the back door. Lindsay shifted, sitting up and edging over to the other end of the swing.

Morgan had a shaggy beard strapped to his head. He danced over to us in tight yellow Speedos and huge sunglasses, singing "Bohemian Rhapsody."

Normally I would laugh—who wouldn't? The guy's an idiot. But Morgan's screwing around was the last thing I needed right now.

Aaron's eyes lit up when he saw me. "Hey! Whassup, Mikey!!" he shouted. He raised his beer. "You too cool for the rest of us down at the fire pit?"

Just then he noticed Lindsay bunched up at the other end of the swing. He looked from me to her, then back at me. Raised his eyebrows.

I rolled my eyes: *Duh!* Aaron's eyes widened in sudden understanding.

He started to back away. "Du-u-ude," he said. "It's cool. We're leaving now." He punched Morgan on the arm and nodded toward us.

Morgan opened his mouth to speak.

"Shut it," said Aaron. "We're leaving." They turned to go.

But it was too late. The door opened again and a group of girls giggled out onto the porch. More people followed.

And my chance was lost.

Titles in the Series

orca soundings